ANXIETY & STRESS MANAGEMENT TOOLKIT

USER MANUAL

Reinhard Kowalski

Winslow Press Ltd
Telford Road, Bicester, Oxon OX6 0TS, UK

Reinhard Kowalski is a Clinical Psychologist and an Accredited Psychotherapist, specialising in the treatment of anxiety, stress and psychosomatic problems. He is particularly interested in combining cognitive therapy and relaxation methods with meditation and self-development approaches. He has written and produced several books and audio products in the area of stress management and relaxation, amongst which are *Over The Top* (Winslow,1987); *Discovering Your Self* (Routledge, 1993) and *Relaxation Tools CD* (Maidenhead, 1997).

First published in 1999 by
Winslow Press Ltd, Telford Road, Bicester, Oxon, OX6 0TS
United Kingdom
www.winslow-press.co.uk

003-4122/Printed in the United Kingdom/1010

British Library Cataloguing in Publication Data

Kowlaski, Reinhard, 1948–
    The anxiety & stress reduction toolkit
    1. Stress management
    I. Title
    155.9'042

ISBN 0 83688 219 6

Table of Contents

Figures

Introduction

This book and cassette pack contains tools and resources for anxiety reduction, stress management and self-development. The techniques, models and exercises are for readers' personal use or for therapeutic work with clients.

I strongly believe that 'working on ourselves' is not only a good thing – it is becoming a vital necessity for individuals, groups, nations, us as a species, the planet and the universe. I admire those people who come to me as clients when they are in crisis. On the surface they want to feel better, to get rid of annoying anxiety or depression. But underneath they are following a soul-call. They want to learn, move on, develop, grow. As a therapist I never know how far I can guide an individual patient – certainly not further than I have gone myself. What I can do is help my patients see their crises as opportunities for themselves and for all of us. That is why all therapy for me is a social and a psychospiritual discipline. Anxiety, panic and stress (including depression) are preventing us from becoming who we really are. Working on those issues helps remove the obstacles on our path.

We are surrounded by many fearful things, people and issues. Fearful things make us anxious. Over the centuries the threats have changed. They used to be wild animals, the weather, enemies, lack of food. Nowadays, in our Western civilisation, the threats have mainly become mental and emotional. Whereas in the past our physical survival used to be threatened, it is now more our psychological, mental well-being that is under attack. However, this can also be an opportunity for our personal growth, for our psychological and spiritual self-development.

The exercises in this booklet and on the cassettes encourage people to make time for themselves. For many, this may be new and unusual. However, persevering with regular quiet relaxation and meditation time will have a beneficial effect on body and mind. All the exercises aim at teaching skills that can also be used in everyday life, so that anxiety-provoking situations can be faced with new strength.

This booklet is divided into four parts, and each part is full of experiential exercises which you can use for yourself or in your work with individuals and groups. Some of the exercises are based on my previous work (Kowalski, 1987; 1993).

I am both a clinical psychologist and a psychosynthesis psychotherapist. In my development as a psychotherapist, teacher and supervisor I have moved from the down-to-earth rationality of behaviourism to the transpersonal realms of psychosynthesis, delving into humanistic and analytical approaches on the way. But I have never rejected my behavioural origins. Personal development inside and outside therapy is about including the previous parts rather than chopping them off. Non-inclusion (exclusion) is what creates the conflicts and drains the energy.

What I am presenting to you in this book and on these tapes is all very practical, mostly based on cognitive-behavioural thinking and working, but throughout I shall also reflect the wider emotional, social and spiritual context, because I strongly believe that essentially we are spiritual beings. In my work as a psychosynthesis therapist I try to include this aspect. So, this book and these tapes are trying to teach you skills as well as trying to inspire you to look beyond everyday reality into the realms of the emotions, of relationship and of spirit.

Part 1 deals with anxiety and panic attacks. Apart from the introduction of psychological models to understand anxiety and panic, there are also exercises and reflections to help overcome anxiety and facilitate self-development.

Part 2 introduces the 'psychological greenhouse' as a model for understanding the widespread and increasing levels of stress in our culture. Ideas about the connections between society, economy and psychological suffering are developed. The main thesis is that our inner psychological space has become so overcrowded that we are losing touch with the important things in life.

Part 3 explores stress management. Again, this part includes exercises that can be used in connection with the tapes. The societal and cultural implications and origins of excessive stress are also explored.

Part 4 contains an introduction to the three tapes and suggestions for their use. In addition readers or therapists need to be familiar with the instructions on the separate photocopiable cards for each cassette before using them themselves or with clients.

Part 1: Anxiety and Panic Attacks

People have written the following stories about their anxiety and panic attacks. They should be read with compassion, and you can compare them with your own or your clients' experiences.

PEOPLE'S STORIES

Richard, *aged 36 years*

It was the last working day before Christmas, during the morning in my London office. I experienced a progressive build-up of strange and unpleasant physical sensations. I left the office to drive home about midday. I felt an urgent need to get home quickly – a sort of panic and loneliness. As I drove out of the centre the physical sensations became progressively worse. It seemed difficult to catch my breath and I had the feeling that something I couldn't control would happen. By the time I reached a town outside London I had to stop the car in a lay-by and found myself walking up and down the grass verge. I kept thinking I was going to collapse. A driver stopped and asked if I was feeling okay. I told him I was not and he drove me to his local general practitioner in the nearby town. The doctor was in and within seconds I had broken down in front of him. I cried for a good few minutes. The doctor checked my blood pressure and did an ECG. No problems with either. He asked what I thought was wrong. I think I replied that everything seemed wrong and I felt the feeling of uselessness and loneliness. Whichever way my mind worked, it was always blaming me for everything. There was a complete lack of confidence and security. The general practitioner gave me 10mg of Valium – I drove home and went to bed early. Most of the symptoms had gone. I did feel very drained mentally.

The same Richard

Months later something very similar happened. Working in my London office during the morning a progressive feeling of losing control of the mind and of concentration developed. I felt helpless and totally insecure. I left the office mid-afternoon and took the underground to Notting Hill

Gate to collect my car. On the tube the build up of tension and difficulties in catching my breath became so bad that I had to get off one stop early at Queensway. I felt the need to get away from people and I walked the rest of the way, trying to pull myself together before driving home. I ended up walking to St Mary's Hospital, where I told them I felt unwell. The doctor saw me and basically went through the same procedure as before. I did not find myself in such an emotional state as before; I was just relieved that someone convinced me that I would be okay – a further 10mg of Valium and off I went in the car, back to my home.

Gillian, *aged 42 years*
My eldest daughter was to appear in a dance sequence at her school. My husband and I were invited to the event. I felt quite calm about going. However, I am always apprehensive about going out. We walked into the school, my husband just ahead of me with my youngest daughter. I looked around, the middle of the hall was empty, ready for the dancing. There were chairs all around the edge for the audience. My legs wouldn't move, I couldn't seem to walk. I tried to call my husband but my voice didn't have any volume. I froze. Fortunately, at this point my husband turned and realised I was in trouble. He came to me. I told him that I couldn't move and that I couldn't face going down those steps to the chairs. He persuaded me to hold on to him and we walked slowly towards our seats. As I walked down the stairs everything seemed to close in on me. I also couldn't seem to focus properly. I became very hot and there was a thumping in my ears. Every pulse in my body seemed to be jumping out of my skin; my legs were like jelly; I was shaking; my heart seemed to be vibrating; my hands were tingling. I felt sheer panic, I would have left then but for my little girl. Fortunately, at that moment the dancing began and as I watched I started to relax and forget about my body and the symptoms gradually went. This happened about a year ago. There have been many school events since and I always feel very apprehensive about attending. I try to face up to each one by relaxing as much as possible and telling myself that there is nothing to fear.

Ian, *aged 29 years*
In June last year I was staying with friends in Hastings. My wife and I decided to go to the horse races at Brighton. On the drive to Brighton I could feel myself becoming very tense. I felt sick, my head was swimming and I remember it being very difficult to concentrate on driving. When we arrived in Brighton we had to park on the seafront and I settled back in the car, trying to relax. I had already taken two and a half mg of Valium that day. Although I felt quite bad I forced myself to drive up to the racecourse. After we parked I got out of the car and found that my legs did not want to work properly. I had to sit down on the wing of my car for a while. When we finally went into the track we sat down away from the crowds and I remember telling myself how ridiculous this all was. As the race meeting progressed, especially when I was immersed in the events, I found I began to feel better. On the drive back I felt much better, apart from being tired.

The same Ian
In early March I was at work and at about 10.30am I was told that a select few were to be taken for a drink by senior management and I, for some reason, was one of those chosen. Immediately I felt an urgent need to visit the lavatory. When I returned I just sat at my desk, the thought of going out being ever present in my mind so that I could not concentrate on anything else. I began to feel sick, became very hot and had to visit the lavatory again. I am not sure but I think I took more than two and a half mg of Valium that day. Once it was time to go, we got together and then had to wait for somebody who was late. As I had to go, I just wanted to get it over with. Once we were on our way I actually felt slightly better. After a stiff double Scotch I began to feel better although I felt somewhat outranked by most people present. I was relieved when it was all over, although I felt somewhat light-headed.

How do these stories affect you, the reader, or how do your clients feel about them? In psychotherapy the emotions the therapist experiences often say a lot about the client. They can be pointers that guide us through the maze of the client's experiences. Usually, the clients are victims of their experiences; and those experiences are often so powerful that they cannot see any structure or sense in them. Our task then is to help the clients develop the ability to become 'observers' of their difficulties, rather than remaining stuck in the position of the victim.

In psychoanalysis this process is called 'counter-transference', where the analyst works with the emotions and thoughts that get triggered in him or herself by the client. The skill of the therapist here is to differentiate between what is his and what comes across to him from the client. It would go beyond the scope of this book to discuss transference, counter-transference and projective identification in more detail. Suffice it to say that these processes are extremely complex, and very powerful when included in the therapeutic process.

EXERCISE 1 Working with your Feelings

1 Remember what you experienced when you read the clients' stories:
What were your feelings towards and about the person?
What thoughts were going through your mind?
What was your reading behaviour? Did you skip through the stories? Did you re-read parts?

Then ask yourself how your experience could be related to the client's experience. If you are reacting to the client's story in a certain way, chances are that other people in the client's environment will react to their story in a similar way. Also you might be experiencing something from 'between the lines' of the stories, something that the client cannot or does not want to experience.

2 What structure do you see in the stories?
Clients, from their victim perspective, are usually not able to see any structure in their experience. It is all chaos, something that just hits them over the head from behind. Hence it can be a valuable starting point to apply some logical structure to the experience.

The following questions could be asked in order to identify a stimulus–response pattern in the available information:

a   *What are the antecedents, the triggers (internal and external) of the panics?*
b   *How is the panic experienced (physically, cognitively, behaviourally)?*
c   *What thoughts, attitudes, mind-sets are connected with the panics?*
d   *What is the outcome of the experience?*

See if you can apply these questions to the stories you have read. Also be aware if you experience resistance to the application of such a structure to people's experience. What is the resistance about? What are you learning about yourself and about the people who have written the stories by asking those questions. (Note that the emphasis here is on the asking of the questions, rather than on the answers, which differs considerably from a purely behavioural approach.)

The exercise *Evaluation* on cassette C, side 1 is a reflection structured in a similar way. By analysing a powerful emotional experience, like a panic attack, in a logical and structured way, the event becomes more manageable and less overwhelming.

BEHAVIOUR THERAPY AS SENSE-MAKING

Reading these stories that were written by some of my clients a few years ago, the overriding feeling that hits me is fear. Anxiety can be seen as repressed excitement, and fear as repressed hostility or anger. There certainly does not seem to be much excitement in the story writers' lives, and I can sense their anger with the roles they have to play.

But in addition I feel desperation and loneliness, and I see little children facing a world that is too big for them. The world in the stories is a cold, demanding world, where the story writers 'have to' function. I sense a lot of internal and external pressure and also an inner emptiness. I am wondering what kind of life those people are leading. They seem stuck and lonely. What are their goals and aims in life? What are their beliefs and values? They seem to be longing for an outer authority that tells them where to go and what to do; and they find that outer authority in doctors or hospitals

(Richard), or in Valium or alcohol (Ian and Richard). Their focus is very much on their physical symptoms: they see themselves as physically ill. It is as if the physical symptoms of panic serve to fill up the inner void by putting adventure and drama into lives that would otherwise be boring and meaningless. Between the lines we can sense something of the emotional conflicts that the physical symptoms are expressing. Richard in particular uses emotional words like 'loneliness, breaking down, uselessness, blaming, lack of confidence' in his story. However, all the story writers are initially looking for solutions to their unpleasant physical symptoms and not for ways of exploring the underlying emotional conflicts.

This is the point where a structured behavioural analysis can be the first step on the path to exploration (see also Exercise 2, p11).

1 Identifying the triggers of the physical symptoms can make the client realise that there are specific situations, whether external or internal, or both, that bring about the symptoms. It also indicates that there are a multitude of other situations that do not cause the symptoms.

2 Analysing the connection between physical sensations and thoughts, self-statements, mind-sets and attitudes, and realising how panic thoughts can cause or exacerbate physical panic sensations can be the client's first step towards a more psychological approach.

3 In general, this behavioural way of 'sense making' can create an important change in attitude. The problem changes to one that can be observed, analysed and understood. The client begins to shift from victim to someone who can begin to exert some control over the problem.

In essence it is the following model that behavioural analysis applies to patients' problems:

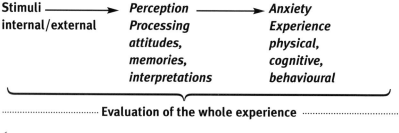

Stimuli ⟶ **Perception** ⟶ **Anxiety**
internal/external   **Processing**   **Experience**
         attitudes,   **physical,**
         memories,   **cognitive,**
         interpretations   **behavioural**

Evaluation of the whole experience

This evaluation of the whole experience then creates the expectations for facing similar situations in future. The whole process consists of conscious as well as unconscious components, and different psychotherapies will address different parts of the process.

FEAR AND ANXIETY: A STRUCTURED MODEL

The flow chart model in Figure 1 of anxiety and panic attacks is quite complex because it tries to explain the connections between all the different psychological elements of anxiety. Please bear with it. Later on in this manual you will find the cartoon story of *Fred and the Banana Skin* which is basically this flowchart in a different form. The chart represents a cognitive model of anxiety and panic attacks. The story of anxiety, panic and stress usually starts with certain life stresses or with the accumulation of those stresses over time (1). At such a time of physical and mental vulnerability, the physical experience of spontaneous anxiety or panic is more likely and it can happen when it is particularly inconvenient, and when the person least expects it, as when driving the car, while shopping or at a social gathering (2). When such a spontaneous panic attack happens to someone who is particularly sensitive and who has the attitude 'I must cope with everything' (3), resulting in high expectations of themselves (4), the panic attack is likely to create a discrepancy between *what is* and what the person thinks *should be* (5). Non-acceptance of the experience can then lead to the 'pull yourself together' attitude (6), which in turn creates more anticipatory anxiety (7). All this is bound to make life more stressful (1), and it can lead to the avoidance of all potentially frightening situations (8), which in itself can lead to further attacks (9). The end result of the vicious circles and the non-accepting attitude can then become depressive self- blame (10), which, again, causes more stress and makes future attacks more likely (1).

Apart from illustrating the importance of thoughts and attitudes, the figure also addresses other issues. The whole process from (1) to (1) can be seen as one big vicious circle, which is made up of two smaller ones, while they are held up by the 'backbone' of attitudes (cognitions): see Figure 2. Vicious circle *A* is the medical/physical one. It starts off with

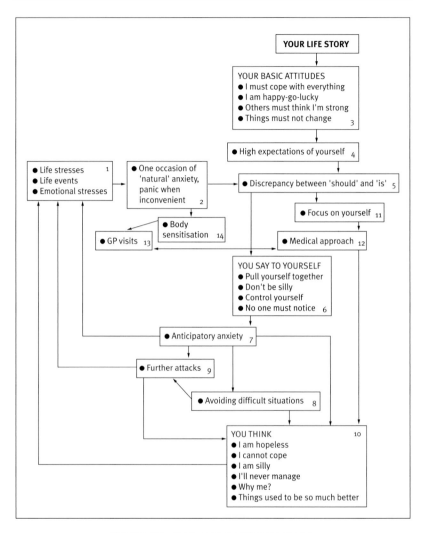

Figure 1 Flow chart: anxiety and panic attacks

people's tendency to focus on themselves and their bodies (11) when they experience a real self-ideal self discrepancy (5). The frightening physical sensations of panic and anxiety are readily interpreted in a medical way as a 'physical illness' (12). Such a medical approach can then

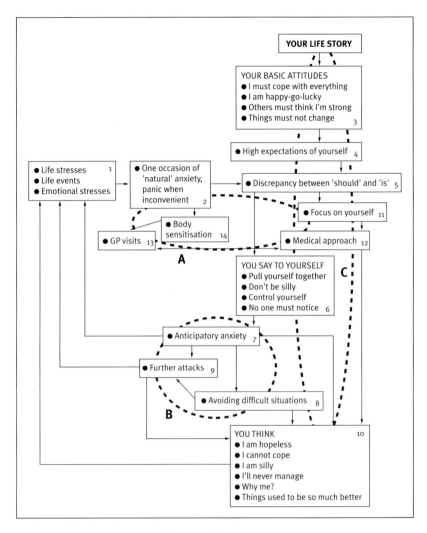

Figure 2 Vicious circles

be further reinforced by visits to the doctor, medical investigations and possibly medication (13). Furthermore, this medical vicious circle is strengthened through the physical sensitisation that takes place as a result of the panic experience(s) (14).

Vicious circle *B* is the avoidance one. It starts off with anticipatory anxiety (7), which causes people to avoid doing certain things or being in certain situations (8). A 'fear of fear' develops. If we then start to avoid driving the car, going into the supermarket or attending social gatherings, the fear of fear tends to grow, because we never put it to the test. When finally, for whatever reason, we face the feared object or situation, chances are that we do so with a considerable amount of tension and autonomic arousal, consisting of our anticipatory anxiety and of the normal startle reaction that happens whenever we face new (or almost new) situations. Thus the conditions for further attacks are ideal (9).

The backbone *C* that energises and maintains the medical and the avoidance vicious circles is the person's attitudes (3, 4, 6, 10). It ranges from perfectionism (3) to defeatism and depression (10). Behaviour therapy and cognitive therapy address the interaction between Medical/Physical (A), Avoidance (B) and Attitudes (C). Different techniques and approaches focus on either A, B or C. Examples of the different techniques and methods, which are explained in the following sections, are:

A: seeing a psychologist/psychotherapist instead of a doctor; applying a psychological model to the problem rather than a medical one; self-observation; behavioural analysis.
B: facing the feared situations/objects; breaking through the avoidance pattern; systematic desensitisation; flooding; *in-vivo* exposure; relaxation techniques to deal with anticipatory anxiety.
C: modifying self-statements; developing a more realistic, more positive attitude; acceptance of what 'is' rather than wasting energy trying to wish it away.

COGNITIVE–BEHAVIOURAL TECHNIQUES

In this section I will invite you to apply to yourself structured cognitive-behavioural techniques in the form of reflections and explorations. There will be one exercise for each of the categories A, B and C. However, the exercises are not 'purely' cognitive-behavioural, but rather they are based in cognitive-behavioural principles, while going beyond it.

Flooding, desensitisation and *in vivo* exposure are the main cognitive-behavioural techniques in the treatment of anxiety and panic attacks. They are all ways of helping the client face the unpleasant situation. In systematic desensitisation this is done in small steps, using relaxation methods to keep the physical fear as low as possible throughout, while in flooding the aim is exposure to the feared situation over prolonged periods of time. The rationale behind flooding is that, physiologically, once the fear reaches its peak it will automatically go down. Avoidance prevents this 'post-peak' experience, and flooding tries to re-create it.

The most immediate relief from panic and anxiety often occurs when a structured psychological model is used in the assessment of the situation. A behavioural psychologist would carry out a 'behavioural analysis'. The following section will take you through analysing a stressful situation in such a way.

The sequence of events

Techniques and methods that fit into this area include the application of a non-medical, psychological, yet structured model to the problem, thus helping clients to assume responsibility for themselves again by including the problem, overcoming a split, an artificial boundary. Behavioural analysis and self-observation charts serve this purpose. The exercise below is the application of a structured, sequential behavioural analysis to an emotion. The sequence is stimulus (stage 1), response (stage 2), consequence (stage 3). The 'three systems analysis' is included by focusing on behaviour, thoughts and physical sensations. The exercise can be useful in the uncovering of 'forgotten' or 'blocked off' experiences. It goes beyond behaviourism mainly in the manner in which the information is pulled together, which corresponds to the 'inner learning' principles of psychosynthesis.

EXERCISE 2 Structured Analysis

This exercise is in three parts. Read each part first, then sit down comfortably, close your eyes and follow the instructions. Keep your body and your breathing relaxed throughout. It will help you remember. Before making notes after each part of this exercise check the instructions to see which parts you may have forgotten. This may give you clues as to where your blocks are. The answers may well be behind the blocks.

Stage 1

Remember a recent occasion when you felt anxious, depressed, stressed or upset. Identify as far as is possible the day, time and location of the start of the feeling(s) by scanning back through time.

Once you have identified the situation when and where the feeling started, vividly imagine yourself in that situation just before the feeling started. Picture yourself, the surroundings, other people, the sounds and smells, the temperature.

Then try and be yourself in that situation.

What was it like to be in that particular situation?
What did you experience?
What were you doing or saying?
What were others doing and saying?
What were your feelings?
What physical sensations did you experience?
What thoughts were going through your mind?
Did you remember something from the past?
Did you anticipate something in the future?

You may find it rather unpleasant to remember everything in so much detail. Or you may find that there are blocks to remembering. Your mind may drift into thinking about other things. Keep your body and especially your breathing calm and relaxed, and gently guide your mind back to the situation.

Once you have explored the context of the beginning of the feelings, see if you can get a sense of what may have been the trigger(s). This may not be very clear-cut, and perhaps it seems as if there was no trigger, as if it all happened 'out of the blue'. If that is the case, focus especially on the things that you did not want to remember, or the things that you had forgotten and only just remembered. Also look at the situation as a whole:

Was the constellation similar to ones that you have found difficult in the past? Is there a pattern that goes back a long way?

Now make some notes about what you have found out about the trigger(s) of those feelings.

Stage 2

Now go back to remembering the situation. But this time focus on your experience of the anxiety, depression or other feeling that you have chosen.

Try and be yourself in that situation. What was it like to be in that particular situation? What did you experience?

See if you can get a sense of what your feelings were trying to tell you. Was it a message from the past? How relevant is that message now? Again, make some notes about your exploration.

Stage 3

Now go to the point in time when the anxiety, depression, or other feeling stopped or changed (if it did). What were the circumstances under which it changed? Did it have anything to do with anything you did, said, thought or felt? Did it have anything to do with other people's actions? Make notes.

Look at the three sets of notes you have made during this exercise and apply the following criteria to them.

1   *What can you learn from the information? How could you summarise the information?*
2   *What is your 'gut reaction' to the notes and the reflection in general?*
3   *Is there an image or symbol for you as a result of this exercise? Draw it if you want to.*

Hidden triggers

The 'behavioural analysis' exercise above is particularly suited to uncovering 'hidden triggers'. These triggers are usually semi-conscious, which means that they can come into conscious awareness with exercises such as the one above.

Example 1

Ian (who wrote two of the stories in the earlier section 'People's Stories' on p3) told us about one of his panic attacks at work. On the day of the Derby he was having lunch at his desk. He then went over to the desk of one of his colleagues, who had a portable television set under his desk, intending to watch the race. Suddenly Ian experienced pressure behind his eyes and a general feeling of shakiness. A dose of a tranquilliser made him feel better. But as soon as the drug had worn off in the afternoon, the panics returned, and stayed with him until he got home.

We went through his experience in great detail, trying to find a trigger. We could not find anything. Then we talked about Ian's holiday, due to start the following week. He was feeling quite apprehensive about it, because he was not only taking his wife and baby daughter, but also his parents and his mother-in-law. He, being the only driver, was concerned about the long car journey to Cornwall, and in general he felt extremely responsible for his family having a good holiday.

Then Ian mentioned quite incidentally that he had phoned his mother from work on the day of the Derby. It emerged that he had phoned her just before he went over to his colleague's desk. Ian then remembered that he had started feeling quite tense when the phone was ringing at his mother's end. She then told him about all the new dresses she had bought for the holiday, and so on. The telephone conversation probably reinforced Ian's rather ambivalent feelings about the holiday.

After the telephone conversation, Ian pushed it all out of his mind. He forgot about it and went over to his colleague's desk and the panics started.

What does the above tell us about hidden triggers?

1 Ian's telephone conversation with his mother connected him with feelings of responsibility for his family, and also with his inability to put himself first. He probably experienced powerful unpleasant emotions, which he tried to push out of his awareness as quickly as possible.

2 Things that trigger panic attacks may be thoughts or feelings that do not fit into the normal course of events. In Ian's case being reminded of his holiday did not fit into his work routine and his excitement about watching the Derby. The telephone conversation with his

mother was therefore not recalled later on, because it did not fit into the logical chain of events at work.

3 Having a panic attack usually means that logical thinking gets impaired. Once it is over we want to forget about it altogether. Our memory of what happened in detail is therefore very limited.

4 In Ian's case, the theme was 'being reminded of a situation where he desperately wanted to cope', that is, providing a good holiday for his family. He did not want to have any negative feelings about the holiday, so he had to deny any negative feelings that were there. This denial of negative feelings can then cause distraction of attention away from feelings, leaving more energy available for attention on the 'body', creating unpleasant physical sensations as a direct result of repressed (non-accepted) negative feelings. The vicious circle of unpleasant physical sensations and more attention being available for those sensations can thus be started.

Example 2

Bill, an airline pilot who had given up flying temporarily because of his panic attacks, described a recent panic experience. It happened while he was standing in the doorway of his home, watching his wife, an airline hostess, dressed in her uniform getting ready to go to work. No trigger was obvious.

Bill was asked to remember vividly everything that had happened at the time, using the above exercise. He then recalled that, just before seeing his wife in her uniform, he had watched a story about an airline crash on the television.

Bill's story seems quite similar to Ian's. He also 'forgot' about an event that probably connected him to rather negative emotions. In this case, it may have been his worries about both him and his wife being in the airline business. In addition to those real fears, it probably also connected him to the fact that he was not able to do his job at the time.

The examples illustrate how a sequential behavioural analysis with its focus on detail, and its inclusion of action, thoughts, feelings and physical sensations, can uncover repressed or 'forgotten' material. The inclusion of such material can contribute to the sense-making process, and it can open the door to looking at deeper emotional issues.

FACING THE DRAGON

The cognitive–behavioural techniques that aim at interrupting vicious circle B are the ones that help people face unpleasant emotions and/or the situations that are associated with those emotions. The fight/flight response is a natural reaction to the experience of fear. We either want to fight an 'attacking' situation, or we want to 'run away' from it. However, the consequences of prolonged avoidance are numerous.

Certainly, one of the most spontaneous and natural reactions to the experience of a panic is the thought 'I've got to get out of here'. This is especially true when the person experiencing the panic is in a shop, a cinema, on public transport or in any other enclosed space. Often this is connected with the overpowering wish to go home or to another place of safety. Leaving the office, getting off the underground, going out of the room for a few minutes, visiting the lavatory – all aim at removing oneself from a frightening and stressful situation. So what is wrong with that, you may ask? Well, in the long run the following paradoxical effects tend to occur as a result of repeatedly leaving the situation.

1 Once the problem situation – shop, office, car, underground – is left, there is usually fairly instant relief from the panic. The experience that 'leaving was worth it', plus the relief from panic, will have been stored in your memory; the action of leaving is reinforced by the subsequent relief from a panic attack. Thus the action of leaving is strengthened as a powerful coping strategy for future panic occurrences.

2 Leaving the situation can therefore easily develop into a bad habit. In future, the slightest experience of panic symptoms can cause the person to run away from situations where even the slightest feelings of anxiety or panic occur. The result is less and less tolerance of panic and fear because the action of leaving has become an automatic habit.

3 After using this coping strategy for a while, the person 'just knows' that certain situations are not for them. And what is the point in going

to the supermarket yet again when you have left it after two minutes the last ten times you went? Out of anticipatory anxiety and a sense of hopelessness, avoidance begins to develop. Certain situations and activities are avoided and more or less good excuses are found.

4 You may by now, quite rightly, feel that the consequences of 'leaving the situation' are rather numerous and far-reaching. The following point adds to the complexity: after a long time of avoiding situations that have in the past been connected with panics, such as supermarkets, trains or being away from home, the avoiding person becomes less and less accustomed to being in those situations. They become strange environments for them. If this person is then, for whatever reason, forced to go into one of those situations, they react to the experience like anyone entering a strange situation – with apprehension and/or alertness. These sensations in themselves can then be the triggers for a full-blown panic attack. And the sad end result of the vicious circle may be the attitude: 'This proves it. I should have known better; I shouldn't have gone into the situation in the first place; I am hopeless.'

Among the most commonly used exercises in cognitive-behavioural work are relaxation exercises. The following exercise uses relaxed breathing as a way of letting go of physical tension, and of preventing hyperventilation.

EXERCISE 3 Relaxed Breathing

This relaxation exercise works best when you listen to it from a cassette. An extended version of this exercise is on cassette A, side 2. The focus of the exercise is to breathe correctly with the diaphragm, thus correcting the tendency to hyperventilate in stressful situations. The exercise also suggest images, and it can help you get in touch with, and through, physical blocks. It can also help you develop a more favourable 'relationship' with certain parts of your body. With regular practice, you will learn to relax rapidly wherever you are.

The numbers in parentheses indicate the pauses in seconds that you should leave if you want to make up a tape using your own voice. Please refer to the section *Using the Cassettes* on p55 of this booklet for instructions about the ideal sitting or lying positions for relaxation exercises.

Close your eyes and concentrate on your breathing. Put your right hand on your stomach, just above your waistline. Now take a few deep breaths – in and out – in and out. Make sure your stomach comes out when you breathe in and that it goes in when you breathe out. Continue breathing regularly and calmly. Push your stomach out a little when you breathe in, and pull your stomach in a little bit when you breathe out. Your diaphragm expands when you breathe in to fill your lungs and it contracts when you exhale. With your right hand on your stomach, just above your waistline, you can monitor that you are breathing properly – filling and emptying your lungs. Try this for a few moments – your stomach comes out when you breathe in and it pulls in when you breathe out. (20)

Also make sure that you don't hold your breath in between breathing in and out. Breathe in continuously and smoothly and then breathe out continuously and smoothly, without holding your breath. Keep your breathing regular and shallow, in and out through your nose. Your stomach expands when you breathe in and it contracts when you breathe out. At the same time, your chest keeps as still and relaxed as possible. (20)

You are now breathing calmly and regularly, and I want you to concentrate your mind on the word RELAX. Say 'RE' to yourself when you breathe in and 'LAX' when you breathe out, still making sure that you diaphragm does most of the breathing work, monitored by your right hand. Say 'RE' when you breathe in and 'LAX' when you breathe out, 'RE' – 'LAX'. And your stomach expands as you breathe in and it contracts as you breathe out. (10)

Keep saying 'RE' to yourself when you breathe in and 'LAX' when you breathe out. Keep doing this and make sure that you don't move your tongue or your mouth when you say 'RE' – 'LAX' to yourself. 'RE' when you breathe in and 'LAX' as you breathe out. (10)

If you are now satisfied that you are breathing correctly, your stomach expanding when you breathe in and contracting when you breathe out, remove your right hand from your stomach area. Remember to put your right hand on your stomach whenever you want to remind yourself to breathe properly. (10)

You may find it helpful to imagine the word 'RELAX' written in huge letters in front of your eyes. Imagine the letters are made from huge blocks of concrete and you are exploring the letters of the word 'RELAX'. (5) Explore the letter 'R'. (10) Explore the letter 'E'. (10) Explore the letter 'L'. (10) Explore the letter 'A'. (10) Explore the letter 'X'. (10) RELAX. (5) And now choose one letter from the word RELAX which could be your favourite letter at the moment. Make up your mind quickly and choose one letter. Imagine that letter in front of your eyes for a few moments. (10)

Remember this letter and the word 'RELAX' whenever you want to remind yourself to relax by controlling your breathing. (10)

With your mind you are now telling your body to relax, allowing tension to flow out with each breath out. And as your body is becoming more relaxed, your mind will also be able to relax more and more. You are using your mind and your breathing to relax your body. This in turn will also relax your mind. (10)

Concentrate again on your breathing and on the word 'RELAX'. Say 'RE' to yourself when you breathe in and 'LAX' when you breathe out. Make sure that your stomach still expands when you breathe in and contracts when you breathe out. (10)

Now concentrate on different parts of your body, breathing into them and letting tension flow out from them with each breath out. Say 'RE' when you breathe in and 'LAX' when you breathe out. (5)

Concentrate on your hands and on your arms. Breathe into your hands and arms, saying 'RE' when you breathe in and 'LAX' when you breathe out. Let tension flow out from your arms and your hands with each breath out. Your hands and your arms are becoming heavy and relaxed. (10)

Now concentrate on your neck. Tell your neck to relax and let all the tension flow out. Say 'RE' when you breathe in and 'LAX' when you breathe out. (10)

Now concentrate on your face and let all the tension flow out from your face. Your face is becoming smooth and relaxed. (10)

Now focus your attention on your stomach. Let go of all the tension in your stomach area. (10)

Now tell your back to relax more and more. You are still saying 'RE' when you breathe in and 'LAX' when you breathe out - no effort at all. Let all the tension flow out from your back. (10)

Now concentrate on your legs. Let go of all the tension from your buttocks down to your toes. (10)

By concentrating on your breathing and on the word 'RELAX' you have allowed tension to flow out of your body. (5)

Now choose one particular part of your body for more relaxation. It may even be an organ or an area inside your body. Perhaps choose a part of your body that you are concerned about at the moment. (10)

Imagine that your relationship with that particular part of your body is rather tense, creating a block or a wall between you and that part. (10)

Try to break through the wall by breathing into that part of your body and letting tension flow out from it. Imagine that the power of your breathing is gradually breaking through the wall, creating a hole though which tension can flow out when you exhale. Continue doing this for a few moments. (20)

And now, slowly and in your own time open your eyes again and be fully alert and awake.

With this exercise, strong emotions can surface. By removing physical blocks, often emotional blocks are also removed. If you do experience strong emotions when you relax your body, try and see this as part of your healing process.

Self-talk

The exercise *Concentration and Positive Thinking* on cassette B, side 2 will help you with controlling your thinking.

In our daily lives we are constantly evaluating situations and ourselves. This process takes place at different levels of consciousness and awareness. In cognitive therapy the aim is to make this process conscious, that is, to put words to it. 'What was going through your mind at the time? What did you say to yourself? What was your attitude then?' are questions that aim at putting words to it again – 'again', because that is how the mental process of evaluation and self-evaluation developed in the first place, before it became unconscious and automatic. The process of 'internalisation' in children has the following stages.

1 Performing an external activity, trial and error, with feedback through the result of the activity.
2 Self-talk (aloud) while carrying out the activity.
3 Self-talk (silent) while carrying out the activity.
4 Wordless inner mental activity while carrying out the external activity.
5 Wordless inner mental activity regardless of the external activity.

The aim in cognitive therapy then, is to 'go back' to stages two and three where the process of evaluation and self-evaluation can be externalised and modified. In a way the whole of psychotherapy aims at this, because it tries to make unconscious and emotional processes conscious by experiencing them and talking about them. I should like to invite you to try a few exercises which are relevant for therapy and which illustrate the points cognitive therapy is making.

EXERCISE 4 Self-blame

What is wrong with self-blame, you might ask. Isn't it better for me to blame myself rather than others? Well, it would probably be best if you could develop an 'objective' attitude towards your problems. But we often hear the following from clients: 'Isn't it silly that I have this problem? I feel so stupid. Everybody tells me there is nothing wrong with me. I really shouldn't go and see my doctor all the time, when he has to deal with all those people who have "real" illnesses.' Does this sound familiar to you?

A similar attitude often develops towards anxiety and panic attacks. Statements like the following are very common: 'I hope no one has noticed.' 'Will I make a fool of myself?' 'Everybody else is so strong, and I am so weak.' It is quite obvious that all of these statements reflect a negative attitude towards yourself. We sometimes call these statements or thoughts 'negative self-talk'. With this we usually run ourselves down, thus making ourselves feel weak and pathetic. And when we feel weak and pathetic about ourselves, we are not exactly in the best position to face anxiety-provoking or stressful situations. Again this makes it all rather complicated, and the following vicious cycle can emerge. You blame yourself for the weakness of having panic attacks. As a result you feel less strong and generally more anxious. Hence you are more likely to experience further anxiety and panic attacks.

Sit down quietly for a few minutes with paper and pen ready.
Now assess how you usually talk about yourself and how you present yourself to people you are close to (family, friends).
What kind of remarks do you make about yourself?
Think back to the last time you talked about yourself to somebody.
Write anything negative and self-blaming you can remember down on the left-hand side of the paper.
And now try to remember how you usually think about yourself and your problems.
What do you say to yourself about yourself? Just think about some of the statements described above, and see if they feel familiar.
Again write down any negative and self-blaming statements that you can identify on the left-hand side of your paper.
Now look at the left side of your sheet of paper. One by one go through all the negative, self-blaming things that you say to yourself and to others about yourself. Change each statement a little so that it becomes more positive.

For example, 'I am just completely hopeless' could turn into 'I am hopeless some of the time, but sometimes I am quite competent'; or 'These symptoms I have mean that I am totally incapable of leading a normal life' could turn into 'These symptoms are a nuisance, but I am now doing something about them.' Write those slightly more positive statements on the right-hand side of your sheet of paper opposite the negative ones. Write down slightly more positive statements even if you don't quite believe in them. Doing this regularly will gradually help you to retrain your thinking, and to develop a more constructive attitude towards yourself.

This exercise uses a 'two column' technique, and is used in one way or another in most forms of cognitive therapy. The important elements are: the verbalisation and externalisation of normally internal and often semi-conscious self-evaluations, and the rational dealing with those usually irrational self-evaluations through trying to find modified and more balanced alternatives. It is then hoped that these alternatives are gradually internalised as new 'mind-sets'. In cognitive therapy questions such as 'How convinced are you of the way you are seeing this?' or 'Can you imagine that someone else would interpret this situation differently?' aim at facilitating this process.

EXERCISE 5 Affirmations

The work with affirmations is not strictly based on cognitive therapy theory, but their usefulness can easily be seen in cognitive therapy terms. Affirmations aim to change attitudes by verbalising the ideal as if it were present reality. They can be a very powerful tool if used correctly, because they aim at directly changing core beliefs. The work with affirmations is based on the theory that they put out an energy that can create or manifest their content. A cognitive therapy explanation would see them as a means of changing someone's attitude towards themselves. This exercise aims at you finding an affirmation for yourself.

Sit down, with your body and mind relaxed, and close your eyes. Imagine yourself operating in the world at the moment, at work, at home, with colleagues, friends and family. And then ask yourself: what core beliefs about myself are operating in my life? Do I usually see myself as succesful, a failure, not good with other people and so on? Make a written list of the core beliefs that you can identify.

Look at the list of core beliefs and identify the most powerful negative one. It may be beliefs like 'I cannot make decisions', 'No-one can possibly like, love or accept me' or 'I don't trust myself'.

Now close your eyes again and reflect upon that one core belief.

Imagine that belief speaking to you. What energy do you feel coming from it?

What is the voice like that is expressing the belief?

What feelings and physical sensations does the belief create in you?

Are there any images or symbols that are connected with it?

Now imagine a voice from deep inside you talking back.

Connect with the qualities of clarity and strength and with your breathing, and formulate the words that could talk back at the belief.

What would that other voice say? Allow that other voice to express the opposite of the core belief.

What energy do you feel coming from that voice?

What feelings and physical sensations does this create in you?

Are there any images or symbols connected with it?

Make notes about your experience with the two voices, and then write your affirmation. Observe the following rules.

1   *Use the present tense: 'I am...' rather than 'I will/could be ...'*
2   *Be positive; state the attitude you wish to create as if it were already achieved.*
3   *Be personal, use 'I' or 'me'.*
4   *The affirmation should establish the image of something already achieved: 'I am ...' rather than 'I will be ...'*
5   *Use action statements, 'I do ...' rather than 'I can ...' or 'I have the ability ...'*

6 *Include your name in the affirmation.*

Work with your affirmation every day. The best times are just before going to sleep and before you start the day. Write the affirmation on cards and pieces of paper and put them somewhere where you will 'run into' them during the day, for example in your wallet or in the car. Visualise the end result as you say, write or read your affirmation. The affirmation will bring up negative emotions. Just acknowledge the emotions without getting pulled into them. Continue working with the affirmation until it has become integrated in your consciousness. You will know that this has happened when your mind responds positively and when you begin to experience the intended results.

Cognitive and behavioural therapies deal mainly with thinking and doing, with the relationships of rational human beings and their relatively predictable environments. Well, that's it then, isn't it? Looks like a good enough model, nice chart, makes sense. Have we got it sussed? The answer, as so many times, has to be 'yes' and 'no'. Critics of the cognitive behavioural model say that it does not include emotions, the unconscious, spirituality, the transpersonal. Behaviourists respond and say, 'But we are scientific, we concentrate on observable behaviours, testing hypotheses, while you are only speculating about things that cannot be scientifically investigated.' The 'tit-for-tat', the 'I'm right, you're wrong' is in full flow: behaviourism is too superficial; psychoanalysis is too wishy-washy; humanistic therapies are too lovey dovey; psychosynthesis is too mystical.

But maybe there is not *one* right approach. Maybe different approaches look at different bits of reality. Even though thinking and doing are the intervention points for cognitive and behaviour therapy, this does not mean that they do not indirectly have an effect on emotions, the unconscious, the sense of higher purpose. On page 7 I used the term 'backbone' for the attitudes and cognitions in Figure 1. When we look up to the sky, we can see the Milky Way as 'the backbone of the night', but we know that what we are seeing is part of an arm of our spiral galaxy. We also know that our (Earth's) position in that galaxy determines what we see. Even our sense that we are looking *up* to the sky is only determined by Earth's gravity: on a larger scale we are just looking *out*. Let us then assume that the vicious circles and the connections within and between them are only parts of larger realities. If we take up that position, what we see might look something like Figure 3.

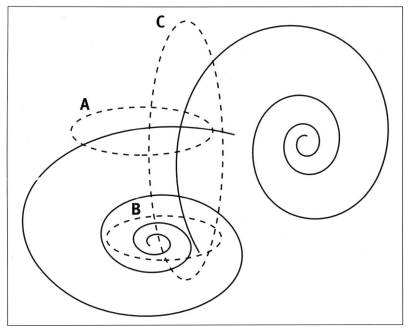

Figure 3 Circles and spirals

GOING BEYOND COGNITIVE–BEHAVIOUR THERAPY

In recent years, cognitive and behavioural researchers have expanded their models to include elements that had previously been ignored, such as the emotions and the unconscious. Information-processing theory and research have particularly focused on the relationship between cognitions (perception and thinking) and emotions. Cognitive-analytic therapy (CAT) is now a well-established school of therapy and includes concepts and models from psychoanalysis. And many cognitive therapists have, no doubt, expanded their approach through their own personal development and learning. Psychotherapy models are not static. They are interactive at all levels, including the personal, the collective and the transpersonal. This does not mean that there are no blinkered and rigid psychotherapists, but you will find them in any school.

I should like to share with you how I see the wider context of cognitive therapy and how it often operates in my practice.

Acceptance

The way I see the wider context of behavioural and cognitive approaches to therapy is as follows. The concept of acceptance, helping our clients to accept where they are at the moment, carries the cognitive-behavioural model into the realms of the emotions and the unconscious. The process of acceptance is the bridge between rational-cognitive and behavioural therapy and a deeper form of guiding patients to discovering their inner world (see Figure 4).

Cognitive and behavioural methods (1) usually aim at change, achieving control over unpleasant sensations and situations, and at

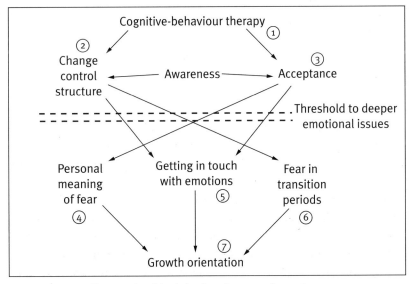

Figure 4 Cognitive-behaviour therapy and acceptance

helping the client to restructure their lives (2). These are the traditionally masculine qualities and skills that most of our industrialised society is based on. The 'official' aims of such therapy seem to reinforce and strengthen the boundaries that we have created in our consciousness between good and bad, happy and unhappy, anxious and calm. At this level, this is not so different from the 'quick fix', the 'happy pills', the systems (for example, medical) and industries that are based on the illusion that happiness and calmness can exist without their so-called opposites. Fortunately cognitive and behavioural methods have a 'side-effect' as well (unfortunately, traditional behaviourists pay little attention to this, as yet). These methods interrupt the vicious circles of avoidance (fear of fear) and medicalisation and thus enable people to face their fear. This usually leads to more awareness and to some degree of acceptance of the fear. It requires courage and fearlessness to face the fear; and where there was only panic and fear of fear, both fear and fearlessness can develop. It is as if through facing the fear, becoming more aware of it, and accepting it more, an original condition (boundary) has been re-created:

```
          fear of fear              panic
A    — — — — — — —     |     — — — — — —

          fearlessness              fear
B    — — — — — — — —   |     — — — — — —
```

Condition A The vicious circles have created a 'higher level', artificial contrast (boundary) between 'fear of fear' and actual panic. Fear can dominate a person's life to such an extent that even when they do not have a panic attack, there is still the fear of having one soon (anticipatory anxiety). Real fearlessness happens only 'by accident' and is hardly noticed, because it is always overshadowed by the fear of fear.

Condition B Cognitive and behavioural methods can help restore a more original condition where fear and fearlessness live side-by-side. However, even in this condition one could still wrongly assume that fearlessness can exist without its opposite. Such a belief can easily create a 'setback' to condition A.

Cognitive and behavioural therapies can go very far and they can also be very limited. However, both achieving control over the problem and accepting that there is a problem to be worked on (3 in figure 4) can lead on to accepting the fact that there are growth opportunities in adversity, that there is strength in the acceptance of weakness, and out of that can develop a willingness to learn from conflict and contradiction (7). Cognitive and behavioural therapies (CBT) can lead to the point of such awareness, but in order to go further into it psychotherapeutically, different models are needed.

The models that can be used beyond CBT in order to go deeper into issues that may have been opened up would cover the following areas, as shown in figure 4:

The personal meaning of fear
After accepting and facing the fear, ask: How has it served you; what did you need to protect; how has it made you strong?

Getting in touch with emotions
Explore emotions other than fear by using fear as a 'link': What is your fear of joy or excitement? How have you learnt to suppress or deal with your sensitivity/vulnerability?

Fear in transition periods
This relates to the specific fears that emerge in transitions between childhood and adolescence, adolescence and early adulthood, mid-life and old age. Often the fears in these transition periods have a very specific flavour. For example, the task in early adulthood is to become independent, to gradually move away from home and to face the world. This needs guidance and preparation. On the other hand, the 'mid-life crisis' is much more a 'crisis of meaning', which often requires the reorientation of attitudes, goals and activities, while at the same time past attitudes, goals and activities need to be accepted and the learning that they have provided needs to be acknowledged.

Part 2: The Psychological Greenhouse

Before exploring stress and stress management, I should like to introduce a model that connects anxiety, depression, stress, alienation, consumerism and fragmentation as cultural and psychospiritual phenomena. In *Discovering Your Self* (Kowalski, 1993) this model is called 'the psychological greenhouse'. Here a summary will suffice to put stress management into its cultural, political and spiritual context.

Cars can serve as a good illustration. The initial motive for building cars was as a means of transport, getting from A to B: increased mobility. Since then the simple concept of the car has been split up into lots of different cars – the flashy car, the fast car, the big car, the safe car, the environmentally friendly car. Each one of those different cars (or aspects of 'car') has acquired its own set of motives and needs, and more needs have arisen out of this split. For example, mobility and speed have become needs in their own right, quite independent of needing to get from A to B for a particular reason. However, all these different needs are connected to a set of basic emotional needs which are often unconscious. The advertising industry has developed the skills and the methodology to link particular aspects of cars with underlying, often unconscious, emotional needs.

It has thus become an aim in production and marketing to split a product up into as many different aspects as possible in order to speak to as many different emotional needs as possible. (For example, the need for 'newness' means that from time to time products are repackaged.) Figure 5 shows how easily the different aspects of the object (circles) can become connected with emotional needs (triangles). The ease of that connection is exploited by the advertising industry. The increasing variety of objects and part-objects created by humanity means that we become increasingly surrounded by 'things' and these things are often connected with deep inner needs. The satisfaction of those deep inner needs then turns into the need for possession of the objects best representing fulfilment of the emotional needs. We become caught up in the vicious circles of needing,

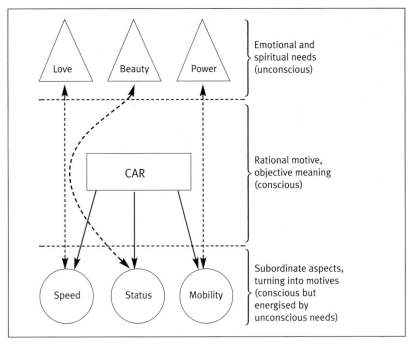

Figure 5 Emotional and spiritual aspects of 'car'

wanting, consuming objects and so on. Thus production not only creates the object for the need, but also the need for the object. All this happens with ever increasing numbers of objects competing for the satisfaction of limited numbers of emotional needs. We are caught up in the 'consumer society': the producers of goods and services and their advertisers are interested in permanently 'hungry customers', and they encourage us, using skilful psychological methods, to believe that our ultimate joy and happiness depend on the acquisition of more goods and more services.

Production also gets pulled into this system: items are invented and produced solely in order to create more variety (as with fashion or electric razors). On the consumption side this system then brings out the shadow side of human nature. Extreme expressions of this include greed, theft, envy, eating disorders, addictions or shoplifting. However, this complex system ultimately leaves the emotional needs unsatisfied. From the system's point of view this is a good thing, because it leaves lots of 'hungry' consumers. At the same time it has turned people in the industrialised world into human beings who project the satisfaction of their emotional needs onto external objects. Emotional needs become 'objectified' to such an extent that many people are not aware of their inner, emotional needs any more. The emotional needs are expressed in the need for consumption. Results are attitudes like 'I want more, greater, bigger things', 'I need to work harder, achieve more things', 'I need to be better than others', 'I need to work, produce more efficiently', 'I need to communicate more quickly' – in short, the 'rat-race'. In the present times of growing global recession and crisis, the needs expressed in these attitudes are becoming increasingly difficult to satisfy. As a result, competition is growing between individuals, groups, companies and nations, while at the same time there is now the opportunity to question and transform the addictive needs the system has created.

Ultimately this situation turns into what I call the 'psychological greenhouse'. We are familiar with the global greenhouse effect, where the incoming heat from the sun gets trapped by gases in the atmosphere, thus leading to rising temperatures and changes in the earth's climate. The psychological greenhouse effect is similar, in that the energies of our emotional and spiritual needs get trapped between the walls of man-made objects that never allow for complete satisfaction or release of those needs.

Many of the stressful situations that govern our lives can be seen in those terms: the endless striving for more and more things and satisfaction; the increasing speed with which we need to do and have it all; the feeling of 'being trapped' and having 'no way out'; the inability to get away from it all. The psychological problems that can be caused by the psychological greenhouse are all the stress-related conditions that we see. Anxiety and panic attacks, obsessive-compulsive disorder and sexual problems can be defined in terms of the psychological greenhouse. It is important to note here that the following definitions of common stress-related problems are not intended to negate their origins in the dynamics of the childhood or other trauma, but rather to show how environmental conditions create a space where earlier trauma is amplified (and even new trauma created) rather than resolved.

ANXIETY, PANIC AND STRESS SYMPTOMS

These symptoms are the result of overstimulation. Everything has become too much. Over a long period of overstimulation and striving driven by fear, fear has finally overtaken and the striver is left behind. The gap becomes bigger and fear takes over more and more. Panic attacks triggered by certain stimuli are the body and mind trying to make sense of it all, thus attaching the fear to specific situations. The situations that fear is attached to usually have to do with too much or too many (people, objects in supermarkets, cars on the motorway), too little or too few (open spaces, loneliness) or the inevitability of death (striving leading nowhere).

OBSESSIONAL RITUALS

Children carry out rituals to structure, to make sense of, a world that is too complex. People in the psychological greenhouse carry out rituals to create their own safe space, protected from the bombardment of objects. Cleaning and checking rituals and the battle against intrusive thoughts can be seen as the individual's struggle against being taken over by the uncontrollable forces around them. Perfectionism, excessive worrying and inability to make decisions are aspects of our disorientation in the face of a world crowded with people, objects and thoughts, and a lack of spiritual guidance.

SEXUAL PROBLEMS

The one area of human interaction where intimacy and union are possible becomes dominated by performance and competition. The need to dominate the partner turns people into objects and ultimately their own sexuality into an object as well. Thus 'objectified', sexuality becomes open to 'market forces': it can be split up, different aspects can be turned into objects, money can be made with it, and ultimately our fears of each other and of intimacy can be turned into something marketable rather than something that sexuality can help us overcome.

Part 3: Stress

Stress has become a very popular topic. Is it just a new trendy thing to be suffering from? Do people use it as an excuse, just to cover up their laziness? Do we all need a certain amount of stress to function; without stress life would be boring? We seem to be so caught up in the belief that life has to be a struggle, that it is common to be rather dismissive about the one shorthand term that describes our dilemma. I should like to see stress as the key term that says a lot about human suffering, fear, the search for sanctuary, alienation – in short, the world we live in.

The following exercise aims at helping you explore the meaning that the word 'stress' has for you. In psychosynthesis, as in other psychotherapeutic approaches, the 'personal' is often used a starting point for learning, rather than more 'general' theories. The danger in the scientific approach (objective rather than subjective) of starting off with a model, and then seeing how an individual fits the model, is that we might cut off important parts of the subjective experience. So let us start off with the 'personal' again, as we started off with people's stories earlier.

EXERCISE 6 The personal meaning of stress

Close your eyes, make sure your feet are touching the floor or ground. Sit upright, but don't overstretch your spine. Make sure your face and your stomach area are relaxed. Now relax your whole body by concentrating on the rhythm of your breathing. Check where in your body you still feel tension, and connect your breathing with those tense parts, breathing into them and letting tension flow out from them with each breath out. Also check what emotions are there for you at the moment, just checking and acknowledging. And have a look at the thoughts that are going through your mind at the moment. See if you can slow your thoughts down, or distance yourself from them a little, so that you are making space in your mind to be able to imagine what I am going to ask you to imagine.

1   *Now consider the word STRESS. What does it mean to you? Just allow thoughts, images, words to emerge.*

    Write down what emerged.

2   *Close your eyes again. Look at your life as it is at the moment; see yourself doing what you're doing in the different areas of your life. When and where and how do you most feel yourself? Imagine yourself doing the things you love doing.*

    Write down what you saw.

3   *Close your eyes again. Look at yourself in the world around you.*

    Look at yourself at home.
    Look at yourself at work.
    Look at yourself in your community, village or town.
    Look at yourself in your country.
    Look at yourself in relation to the world.

    What is your relationship with the world around you? When, how and where do you feel connected to the world around you? When, how and where do you feel disconnected from the world around you?

    Make notes.

4   *Read through all your notes and be aware of your physical sensations and of your emotions as you do so. Then close your eyes again. Calm down the signals you are receiving from your body, your feelings and your thoughts. And then connect your feelings with the material that you have just written down. Allow a symbol, an image or a statement to emerge.*

    Make a drawing of the symbol or image that you saw or write down the statement that came up.

    After this exercise you should have some sense as to where you are in relation to stress and the world around you. Take your symbol, image or statement away with you into your everyday life and use it to become more aware of yourself, your stress and your relationship with the world around you and within you.

Earlier we defined the 'psychological greenhouse system' as one of fragmentation and separation. This applies to our relationships with ourselves, with others and with our environment. Perhaps you would like to consider your experience of the above exercise in this context: do you feel less stressed when you feel connected, and do you feel more stressed when you feel disconnected?

When we say 'I am stressed' we are looking at the surface only. Underneath are internal and external boundaries, alienation and 'greenhouse' issues. A major area of (di)stress is the inherent and increasing confusion between means and goals. Mobility, for example, used to be the means for a goal – to get from A to B. Now mobility has become a goal in itself and new means (holiday resorts, transport, roads and so on) have been developed in order to satisfy the need for mobility. A similar confusion is true for food, clothes, houses, furniture and so on.

Being caught in the psychological greenhouse means that we are disconnected from the earth (which we see as a 'thing' to be exploited) and the heavens (which we see in 'heavenly' goods, relationships or pursuits). This disconnection from heaven and earth, plus the rigid boundaries at all sorts of levels with the dissolution of boundaries happening at the same time, create the general 'greenhouse' conditions and the associated psychological distress. At the same time we have been born into and are developing in an increasingly complex and fragmented human world. Inevitably the process of internalising the environment leaves many areas about which we know either nothing or very little. Many things we only internalise in extremely abbreviated and symbolic ways. There is always more 'not-knowing' than 'knowing'. Consequently we are all the time faced with the 'fear of the unknown', which creates a basic level of fear and also causes us to block off the terror of the abyss that we are facing daily. On the positive side, somewhere along the line, at least some of us should by now have developed the ability to deal quite well with facing the 'unknown'.

The 'psychological greenhouse' means that 'sense making' is becoming increasingly difficult. If we cannot make sense of our environment, our relationships, our goals, our feelings and values, it creates stress. So, in order to find some structure in chaos and disorientation we often need to revert to our basic biological survival mechanism – the flight or fight response – which then shows itself as anxiety and stress.

Before moving on to exploring more traditional stress management procedures, the following exercise invites reflection on a particularly powerful mind-set, the belief that life has to be a struggle.

EXERCISE 7 Life is a struggle

How much do you believe that life has to be a struggle ?
How much has the belief that life is a struggle influenced you in your life ?
Scan your life story for this.
How is this belief serving you now ?
How is this belief hindering you now ?
What is your reality now ?
How much do you struggle out of survival necessity and how much do you struggle out of an old belief system ?

Imagine what it would be like to find your identity without struggling.
Visualise, write or draw what it would be like.
What energy can you feel in that visualisation ?

Stress Management

It has become quite acceptable and trendy to talk about stress and about its management, about 'coping with life', about having a rational approach to our problems, about thinking more positively. Earlier we explored the deeper issues that are underneath it all. Let us now look at the more 'rational' approaches to stress management.

Stress management is often sold in 'packages', and the approaches generally are very rational and very structured. They teach you about structuring your life differently – from healthy eating, giving up smoking, more exercise and less boozing to more relaxation, positive self-talk and even meditation. Two points need to be considered here.

1 Increasing numbers of people are going to their doctors and their psychologists to ask for help with their experience of stress. It seems to be becoming acceptable to do this. 'I am suffering from stress' seems to be developing into a symbolic expression of 'There is something wrong with me and with my world. I feel wrong and my relationship with my world, with my life feels wrong. My body is expressing this with stress symptoms.' The statement 'I am suffering from stress' seems to have become a shorthand way of saying the much deeper things about our inner and outer world for which we do not have quite the right words.

2 While some companies offer training in stress management for their employees, others still regard stress as a 'dirty word'. If you suffer from stress symptoms, you are really saying 'Something is wrong. I don't like it.' Such a statement is not readily acceptable in our performance-oriented business world. Chances are that you, the sufferer, will be regarded as not being 'good value for money'. Your stress will most likely be seen as your personal failure to meet the demands that others seem to be able to meet without any problems. As a result people often struggle on, trying to get through their stress symptoms until it is too late. On the other hand, there are a number of companies which give their employees some training in stress management, offer counselling or refer people on for individual counselling. Obviously, in recessionary times both tendencies will be very evident: the reluctance to spend money on stress management; and the concern to keep the remaining workforce as sane and productive as possible.

It is unlikely that companies would be interested in exploring with their employees the deeper issues behind stress, as I have described them earlier. However, even very superficial stress management, such as superficially applied behaviour therapy, can open the door to deeper issues. Therefore let us look at what could be relatively 'safely' used by companies without directly and immediately turning their employees into 'new age warriors'.

Standard stress management sees stress very much like a mechanistic term from physics. It means that one object is exposed to the force of another object. When the force of the second object is equal to or greater than the resistance of the first, the strain put on the first object will eventually break it. It is a 'battle' between two objects, with the stronger surviving. Hence traditional stress management has focused on three issues.

1 The analysis of the strengths of object A (the individual and their ability to withstand pressure) and object B (the environment and its capacity to exert pressure). The 'general adaptation syndrome' considerations represent such an analysis.

2 How we can strengthen A to withstand more pressure from B. Relaxation, meditation, a healthy diet and exercise all aim to strengthen physically A. In addition it has been found that A's perception of B, that is, the extent to which A perceives B as a threat, determines the actual physical stress response. This is also related to the question why two different individuals would be stressed to different degrees by exactly the same situation. Cognitive therapy methods are employed here to analyse and modify an individual's perception of being threatened by B. What is being threatened and why? Is my interpretation of the situation realistic? What is the worst that could happen? It is easy to see how asking questions like this can lead to asking a more basic question: What do I really want out of life and does my work/home life still give me what I want and need? This is the 'cutting edge' of stress management, the point at which it can turn into deeper questions about goals, meaning and values. While companies are interested in having stronger, more stress-resistant employees, they are obviously not interested in having employees who put energy into working on their goals and values, because such work will inevitably also lead to a questioning of the meaning of work, the culture and the values of the company, and the type of relationships at work.

3 How we can make B less stressful. This is a very delicate subject, especially when it comes to the work environment. Obviously, a lot of things can be changed to make the work environment less stressful: changes in the physical work environment, improving communication, changing management styles, changing work allocation systems, giving employees the opportunity to express themselves. However, there is one boundary which these changes cannot cross: the competitiveness of the company. Therefore, employees' productivity, motivation and loyalty

must not become impaired. But what happens to those employees who become more aware of themselves and their environment and who then might also become aware of the 'growth terror' and the alienation that dominate our personal, social, economic and political lives? How could somebody like that still work in financial services or in marketing? The question then becomes: can consciousness remain limited in stress management; can we become more critical without beginning to question the system within and without?

Stress Management Workshop

Most of the available stress management techniques are based on behavioural and cognitive therapy and they try to establish a clear cause-and-effect relationship, whereupon programmes are designed that modify the identified causes, reactions and attitudes. Such programmes can be very useful in the same way that cognitive–behavioural methods can be very useful (see 'Going Beyond Cognitive–Behaviour Therapy' on pages 26–29). The fact that these programmes can open up deeper levels applies as well. Ultimately, they may afford participants glimpses into the issues around growth and alienation, and uncomfortable questions might be asked. This is similar to the 'job-enrichment programmes' that were carried out in Detroit in the 1950s. There, experiments were tried to make the jobs of assembly-line workers in the car manufacturing industry more interesting. Work groups were formed which produced a whole car from beginning to end rather than each worker performing the same repetitive task day after day. It was found that the productivity of the work groups was higher than the productivity of the assembly-line workers. However, there was a side-effect as well. The work groups were also beginning to become more interested in overall company issues. It was as if, once their range of activities and therefore their range of consciousness was expanded to the car as a whole, they also wanted to become more involved in the running of the company as a whole. Obviously, this would be rather uncomfortable for a system that relies on control through hierarchies, division of labour and powerlessness of the workforce. Consequently the experiments were stopped because they were threatening the system.

I think the same must be true of any activity that tries to expand consciousness, whether it is behavioural, cognitive or aimed at stress management. The economic growth system relies on the maintenance and the heating up of the psychological greenhouse, and any greater degree of awareness or consciousness is likely to throw up other, more fundamental questions in people. Therapists must be aware of this, so that they can do their job in a responsible, careful and compassionate way.

I have used the following exercises in stress management training. I think they are good examples of the ways in which structured exercises can open up deeper psychological realms. The exercises are presented here as a resource, either for you to use yourself, or to use in your work with others.

STRESS MANAGEMENT EXERCISES

EXERCISE 8 Fred and the Banana Skin

The following story, Fred and the Banana Skin (taken from *Over the Top*, Winslow, 1987) contains all the elements of the rather complicated flow chart on page 8 in narrative form. Used as an experiential exercise it addresses less intellectual and more emotional ways of processing. Read Fred's story with an open mind and heart, and see what it does to you.

This is the story of Fred. He is a bit of a perfectionist – he likes doing things well. Occasionally he gets nervous, but not too nervous. In the back of his mind he thinks to himself: 'I must be seen as coping well with life. I am just happy-go-lucky. Things could go on like this forever.'

However, deep down Fred is quite soft and vulnerable, although he would not normally admit to this. One day, as he is going about his business, he feels a bit tired. There are problems with the car, a few things at work and

the flu he's just had. He doesn't notice the banana skin right in front of his left foot.

Fred steps onto the banana skin, stumbles and falls. Suddenly the ground is taken from underneath him – he is upside down.

The fall has really frightened Fred. His heart is beating extremely fast, he is trembling and he is getting hot and cold. And being the sensitive person he is, he is very upset about his mishap. Suddenly the world seems very strange and not the same any more.

'Hope this won't happen again. Hope nobody saw me,' Fred thinks to himself. But his heart is beating so fast, and there is the trembling – better go and see the doctor. More aware of his body than ever before, he stumbles into the surgery. The doctor checks him over: 'You're fine, nothing to worry about. It's just your nerves, a

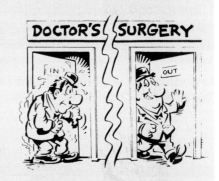

stress reaction.' Fred is reassured and he leaves the surgery feeling better. But he is still a bit worried, mainly about his heart and about banana skins.

Fred is now feeling quite reluctant to go anywhere near the area where he fell. In fact, even thinking about going there makes his heart beat faster. 'This is silly,' he says to himself, 'I must pull myself together.' But just to make sure, he is beginning to watch his step, carefully looking around

corners. And one day it actually pays off – he is quite certain that there was this huge banana skin waiting for him just around the corner. Or did he just imagine it? Fred worries: 'Maybe I'm going mad. What will people think of me?'

Fred is now beginning to avoid more and more situations and places where he thinks there could possibly be a banana skin. He is imagining them everywhere – on buses, trains, in supermarkets. He is thinking about banana skins a lot of the time; and a lot of the time he is slightly anxious, his heart beating fast and his hands trembling. Fred sighs: 'I wish things were the way they used to be; I was so strong and happy. Why has all this happened to me?'

Through fear of banana skins, Fred is now becoming quite reluctant to leave the house. But even indoors he feels anxious. He thinks: 'Maybe I'm ill. Maybe I should go to see the doctor. After all, he helped me last time.' But just the thought of leaving the house, makes his heart beat so fast, and he trembles all over. Fred imagines that there is this huge banana skin waiting for him right on his doorstep.

First of all check what your emotional, physical and rational reaction to Fred's story is. Now make two lists of five of your own banana skins, both at work and outside work.

Consider how much these banana skins are influencing your feelings, your thinking and your behaviour. To what extent have you, like Fred, blown up the dangers out of all proportion? There may be deeper reasons for this. On the other hand, there may not, and all that has happened has been the operation of the vicious circles that we discussed earlier. You can now begin to question your anticipation of danger by asking how realistic your fears really are.

EXERCISE 9 Analysing a Stressful Situation

This exercise is based on the behaviour-analytic approach described earlier. It will help in the first stages of 'sense making' and the benefits are thinking about the exercise, beginning to see connections, talking about it, accepting it, beginning to have feelings about it. The *Evaluation* exercise on cassette C, side 1 is similar.

Think back to a recent stressful situation. Identify the day, time and place and imagine what happened as vividly as possible. Make notes:

1 *How and when did the situation start?*
2 *Who was saying/doing what?*
3 *What did you do and say?*
4 *What thoughts were going through your mind at the time?*
5 *What feelings were there at the time?*
6 *How did the situation stop being stressful?*

Look at the sequence of events and ask yourself: at what point(s) in the course of events could I have said, done or thought something different in order to make the situation less stressful? (The exercise, Preparation, on cassette C, side 2 can be used for this.)

EXERCISE 10 Body, Feelings, Thoughts

(This is a shortened version of the *Meditation* exercise on cassette B, side 1.)

Sit in a relaxed position with both feet on the floor, upright, but not strained. Close your eyes and connect with your breathing. Then be aware of all the physical sensations you can. Do not change anything, just check all your physical sensations.

Now focus your attention on your emotions. What emotions are inside you at the moment? Again, try and be a detached observer of your emotions. Don't become overinvolved with any of the emotions that are there. Just check them and acknowledge them.

Now move your attention to the thoughts that are going through your mind. Watch the thoughts and images that are going through your mind. Be aware that the thought, 'I am not having a thought' is a thought as well.

Ask yourself (a) How does my body usually experience stress? (b) What emotions do I experience when I am stressed? (c) What thoughts are going through my mind when I am stressed? Make notes about your observations or, if you use this exercise with a group of clients, have a group discussion using the questions.

Exercise 10 introduces the concept of 'disidentification', which is one of the standard procedures in psychosynthesis. It assumes that experience can be divided into physical, emotional and mental aspects. It also assumes that we can learn to go into an 'observer position' in order to just observe the body, the feelings and the mind, rather than being completely caught up in one or two of these areas of our experience. It can be extremely useful to develop the ability to be able to look at experience from the observer position, because often our whole identity gets caught up in a physical sensation, an emotion or a thought. Three examples of this are given here.

1 In panic attacks all the attention is focused on the physical sensations of panic. Vicious circles can develop between thoughts and physical sensations (see the cognitive-behavioural model of anxiety and panic that was developed earlier on): panic sensations trigger panic thoughts

– panic thoughts increase the panic sensations – more panic thoughts – more panic sensations. It is interesting here to note that most people with panic attacks are quite unaware of their emotions. One could say they have learnt to 'repress' their emotions. Usually the emotions concerned, such as anger or excitement, are ones that have become traumatised in childhood. It is as if the body is still expressing the emotions in a physical way, and the mind tries to make sense of it, but cannot gain access to the repressed (hidden away) painful emotional content and context (this is also related to our earlier discussion of 'hidden triggers'). Disidentification offers a way of stepping out of those vicious circles by developing an attitude such as 'My body and my mind are panicking again. I wonder what this is all about?' However, this may not be sufficient to enable access to the repressed emotional content and context. But it will strengthen the awareness of a centre that is beyond our usual areas of experience (the observer, the self).

2 In depression, the focus is on one emotion only. Again, this exclusive focus can be a defence against other, even more painful, emotions. Disidentification can redress the balance by developing an attitude such as 'This feeling of depression is there again. I wonder what other feelings are there or were there.'

3 With obsessive-compulsive ruminations (worrying) the focus is on the thoughts, again possibly as a defence against painful emotions. An observer-like attitude would be 'I know that my mind is worrying again. I wonder what emotions and physical sensations are or were there.'

In stress management, this connection with the self can lead to the creation of the 'inner sanctuary' from which both the internal and external world can be approached differently. As we have discussed earlier, such a different approach can easily include the questioning, not only of inner psychological patterns, but also of the world around us. For example, the question becomes whether companies, who are caught up in growth pressures and competition, can really afford employees who are critical and questioning. The answer is yes, as long as stress management increases creativity and productivity. But what about the 'side-effects'?

EXERCISE 11 The Tyranny of the SHOULDS

This exercise aims at changing 'mind-sets'. These are our attitudes, beliefs, assumptions, prejudices and stereotypes that help us make sense of our experience. Our brain without mind-sets would be like a computer without software. We need mind-sets to process all the incoming information. These cognitive structures can become very rigid because they have developed over a long period of time, often from early childhood. We then hang on to them as if it were a matter of life and death, even though the particular way of seeing things may not serve us any longer. The result is rigid boundaries that make it impossible for us to see things from a different perspective. We can approach those mind-sets in two steps:

1 *We first need to become aware of which mind-sets are operating in a particular situation. Then we have to ask ourselves, 'How does this mind-set serve me, and how does it limit me?'*
2 *And then we need to ask 'To what extent am I the master of this mind-set, and to what extent am I its victim?'*

Important mind-sets are the 'shoulds' that we carry around with us. They are our rules for living. Without thinking about it for too long, see if you can make a list of your 'shoulds', by completing the statement 'I should ...' ten times.

It does not matter if you wrote down fewer than ten 'shoulds'. It can help to rank the shoulds in order of importance or strength.

 Now take a large sheet of paper and some coloured pens to draw your map of 'shoulds'. Start off with the most important or strongest 'should' and draw a circle on the paper, with size and colour reflecting importance and strength. Write the 'should' inside the circle. Then take the next 'should' and place it in relation to the first one, in terms of distance, size and colour. In this way, put all your 'shoulds' on the map. You can also connect the circles with lines, thick, thin or dotted to indicate connectedness or lack of it. Some of the circles may overlap, others may be totally disconnected.

 Look at your map and take in the structure on paper. What does it look like? What does it feel like? What energy do you feel coming from the map? How does the energy relate to your experience of stress?

If you are doing this exercise in a group, get together with one other person, and let that person be your counsellor. Show them your map and let the other person interpret it for ten minutes. Just listen to the way another person sees it. Then swap roles.

As a last step, go back to your original list of 'shoulds' and read them out aloud once – slowly and with an awareness of what each one feels like. Then go through the same list again, replacing 'should' with 'could'. What does that feel like?

Something else you can do with your map is to stand on it with your eyes closed. What does it feel like in your body? Feel the energy from the 'shoulds' in your body and let your body take on the posture of the map. Be aware of all the sensations and feelings in your body as you do this. Then step outside the map and stand on the floor or ground. What is it like? Take on the body posture of being away from the 'shoulds'. Be aware of feelings and sensations. Then step back onto the map, and off it again. Become aware of the dance between the two positions.

Make notes about your experience with this exercise, if you are in a group, share your experiences.

BEYOND STRESS MANAGEMENT

I have earlier defined the statement 'I am stressed' as an expression of deep distress in our inner and outer world. What does it then mean to uncover the deeper dissatisfaction and dis-ease that is underneath the top layer of 'stress'? What happens when we glimpse the stress and pressure that surround us worldwide, or the confusion between means and goals, or the alienation from our values and purpose? In short, what do we do once we want to clear the space surrounding us of all the objects – objects that have imprisoned us, but have also given us a sense of security?

I have no clear answer to the questions, but I would like to develop some guidelines for our journey. Perhaps guidelines are too ambitious, perhaps this sounds rather like aiming at a grand finale. Perhaps if I aim at enabling you to become a little more aware of your journey in the greenhouse, you may be able to come up with your own individual guidelines to suit your particular journey.

Stress Story: the Therapist

Often nowadays when I run groups and see individual patients I can clearly see how their particular problems are related to 'greenhouse issues'. However, my training as a clinical psychologist and as a psychotherapist has not prepared me to deal with this. I can focus on the intrapsychic, and interpersonal dynamics, the transference and counter-transference, but what do I do when I can so clearly see them as rats in the Skinner-box of our systems – conditioned, trapped, limited, their human potential so crippled in terms of sensitivity, creativity and transcendence that it is hardly recognisable. What do I do with the pain and anger that I feel then?

I can help people on their journey, can bring them to the edge of seeing, but I cannot yet show them the safest way through the unknown territory beyond the greenhouse, because I myself am standing on the edge of it, scanning and searching for a reasonably safe path. Maybe there is no 'reasonably safe' path? It does feel as though action beyond being a psychotherapist is needed. Maybe it is easier to be cynical, or to think that it is all people's own responsibility, or to think that at least with a psychiatric or psychological diagnosis and appropriate 'treatment' we can make people feel better. But how can I still live with that, when I can hear my patients' screaming, echoed by the walls of the greenhouse? Can I still be content with the fact that I hear it, but they do not?

Stress Story: Peter

Peter, aged 52, has just had major surgery and completed four months of chemotherapy for cancer. The scans are now clear, but the cancer is a recurrence of 20 years ago. He is American and he has been living in Britain for four years. He is a sales manager for an American firm and he went back to the States for his chemotherapy. His placement in England ends in two months' time and he has to decide whether to stay on for another year or not. His industry has been badly hit by the recession. If he goes back to the United States his job security is not very good. He could take early retirement, but he could not live on his pension. If he stays in Britain, he will miss the birth of his grandchildren (twins) in the States and he will still have to go back in a year's time. He does not like his job any more, he is unable to make up his mind, he cannot concentrate, he sleeps badly, he worries all the time; he is stressed. He has always been a worrier, but he thinks he should be happy. He gets panic attacks and he cannot relax, and he experiences a lot of guilt about things in his past. He worries so much that he often gets a tight feeling around his forehead and his temples.

I can see that Peter is very needy. He wants me to tell him what to do. I feel uncomfortable with taking the responsibility for his decisions, but at the same time I desperately want to help him. I am beginning to realise that Peter's present pressures are bringing up for him all the insecurities from his childhood – the fact that he never knew his father, who left when he was a baby, and that his whole childhood was cold and unsupportive. I am beginning to feel enormous pressure to help Peter, knowing that I probably have only one month to work with him. I know that the pressure I feel is similar to the pressure he feels. I am trying to do my best, knowing that I would need at least a year to get anywhere near the real issues. After four sessions Peter fails to turn up for any further sessions with me. I feel helpless and I am beginning to realise that Peter must be carrying a lot of anger in himself, and that he has probably proved to himself again that nobody can help him.

Stress Story: Michael

Michael used to be a top marketing manager in a financial services firm. He is now 43, is married, has two adolescent children, a big house and a big mortgage. Four years ago Michael's wife became depressed and she received medication treatment and psychotherapy. Cracks in the marriage became more obvious and Michael's wife began to criticise his behaviour: his excessive working hours, his constant exhaustion, his inability to express his feelings and his often autocratic behaviour at home. Michael took heed of his wife's complaints and went into therapy himself. He learned to be more aware of his feelings and to express them more. He also began to see how his extreme ambitiousness was still driven by 'little Michael' desperately trying to please his father. He was becoming increasingly dissatisfied with the coldness and falseness of communication and interaction at work. Michael's colleagues and superiors were noticing that Michael was 'different', he seemed 'softer', occasionally he would become tearful at work.

During a restructuring exercise at work Michael was 'side-stepped' and some of his responsibilities were taken away from him. His resilience and his ability to deal with stress were being questioned. At the same time, Michael was increasingly doubting his motivation for his work. Eventually, he resigned from his very highly paid job. He experienced an enormous sense of relief and freedom, but at the same time fear set in. He was feeling empty, worthless, useless, and he was desperately trying to make plans for the future, ranging from setting up his own horticultural business to doing private marketing consultancy work. The fears were interfering with the creative space he had made. Michael was bringing all this to my men's group, where others were dealing with similar issues to do with their newly discovered craving for personal growth, as opposed to the performance pressures of career, mortgages and so on – in short, society's growth madness had turned personal.

Is this, then, the ultimate, inevitable result of stress management? People who can no longer conform to the 'normal' rules and demands, but who still have to pay their mortgages and car loans? What are the alternatives, the niches? Should all of the more aware people work for 'green' businesses or charities? Should we all sternly refuse the demands and temptations of this seductive system and get out of it? Where would we go? Are there alternatives 'out there'?

Michael then visited the Findhorn Community, a spiritual community in the north of Scotland, for a week in order to experience different ways of working and living together. He did the 'experience week' and came back full of the spirit of Findhorn. He started telling me his story by saying how upset he had been that he had forgotten to take his group photograph and address list when he left to come back home. 'I have never felt so close to a group of people in my life. When I got back I felt so empty.' He then proceeded to tell me about the last session of the week, called 'completion', where everybody just talks about their experience of the week. In accordance with an old American Indian habit, a stone is passed around from the person who speaks to the one who should speak next. At the end of the five-hour sharing of experiences, the question arose as to who should take the stone home. Four people said they wanted to take it. As the group set about trying to decide who should be given the stone, something in Michael suddenly told him that he wanted it. The reason was that he felt there was so much *love* in it, because everybody was holding it as they were speaking. In the end, he got the stone, together with the experience that he had, for the first time in a long while, asked for something for himself. He had used his courage for a purpose reaching beyond greed.

Stress Story: Ormond Stores

Staying in the cottages near Ballypatrick in County Tipperary, I drove to a small country shop/one-pump petrol station to buy a few bits and pieces. In my usual 'civilised' manner, I already had plans for the rest of the afternoon in my head: there was a 'leisurely' pint to be had in the pub in Ballypatrick; there was Slievenamon, the mountain to be climbed before going back to England in two days' time; there was dinner to be prepared, and so on. All in all, the shopping trip was a nuisance; there were other, more interesting, more important things to be done, to be achieved. Hence the plan was to spend as little time as possible in the shop. However, I got chatting to the woman owner behind the counter after buying my items. We talked about England and Ireland, young people leaving Ireland to get hold of all the glossy things 'over there', but then wanting to come back because they couldn't find 'it' over there either.

I was enjoying the natter, but there was also that little voice somewhere inside that said that I should be moving on now. And as I was talking and looking at her across the counter, my eyes were attracted to some red cardboard boxes behind the cash desk. They contained batteries. Suddenly I remembered – I had wanted to buy one 'AA' battery, but had forgotten about it. I bought it and told the woman the story of how I had almost forgotten it. 'Normally' I would have rushed into the store, bought my things, my mind already dealing with things ahead, and I would probably have noticed that I had forgotten to buy the battery in the car on the way back. I would then have turned the car around, driven back to the store, by then being in a terrible rush, bought the battery and rushed on again.

Wasn't this a much more pleasant way of being reminded? And, efficiency-wise, the relatively relaxed chat probably required less energy, hustle and risk taking than the racing back and forth in the car would have done.

The four stories above suggest ways of dealing with stress in a wider context. They range from the 'simple' solution of slowing down to facing the need to 'get out of the rat race'. I strongly believe that, once we begin to work on our stress problems, we sooner or later will face those two issues: slowing down and somehow stepping out of the greenhouse. Many people will not face these dilemmas in their lifetime. Others will be able to stretch out the preliminaries, such as learning to relax more and learning to communicate better, so long as they never come to the edge. Others, like Peter, will carry lots of repressed emotions through their lives, without finding or accepting the opportunity to release them, but will instead develop physical illnesses. Many, however, will be standing there on the edge, like the therapist and Michael.

ROUNDING OFF

This book and the accompanying cassettes try to provide you with material, exercises and ideas to find a way into your own or your clients' anxiety, panic and stress problems. In addition, the written and spoken material aims to help you on the path of self-development because, once we start working on our problems, we begin to explore ourselves, others, life, the universe and everything. It is this 'interconnectedness of everything' that is emerging in psychology, philosophy and other areas of science such as quantum physics. This book therefore addresses anxiety and (di)stress at different levels, from the very concrete, practical behavioural to the more general societal, philosophical and spiritual. The 'Further Reading and Listening' list at the end also reflects these different levels.

For you or for your clients it is important that you use the problems as an opportunity, as a starting point for the journey of self-discovery. It does not matter so much where and how you start. Once you have made the first step, even though it may initially be difficult to face your problems, you will be on a journey of learning and of change. That is what life is all about. Good luck!

Part 4: The Cassettes

Please study this information carefully before you use the cassettes for yourself or with your clients. The exercises on the cassettes contain powerful psychological techniques and should be used with care. If you use the cassettes with other people, make sure that you are familiar with the exercises. Practitioners must ensure that cassettes are only given to clients with the written instructions. Important detailed information about each exercise is on the separate photocopiable cards.

USING THE CASSETTES

Throughout this booklet it has been emphasised that the experience of anxiety and stress, apart from being unpleasant, also presents opportunities for people to learn about themselves and to change their lifestyles. The three cassettes in this pack aim to teach a range of relaxation and meditation exercises and skills for self-development. They contain six different self-help exercises, each of which concentrates on a particular aspect of anxiety, tension and stress. Each exercise includes a physical relaxation induction which, as well as being useful in its own right, also facilitates better concentration on the exercise instructions. The six exercises can be used as a programme, or individual exercises can be used for specific purposes. In the text of this booklet I have referred to some of the exercises. Here I should like to introduce you to the cassettes in more detail.

You can do the exercises in either a sitting or a lying position. Those exercises which teach you skills that you want to use when you are out and about you should practise in a sitting position at least sometimes. Also take into account that meditation is usually practised in a sitting position.

Ideal Sitting Position

The best and most comfortable position for relaxation and meditation is sitting upright with your back and head as straight as possible without tension. Pull your shoulders back slightly and push your chest out a bit.

Put your chin up a little. Have your hands on your lap with your palms facing up or with one hand cupped in the other. Have your legs uncrossed and be aware of the contact of your feet with the ground. Most importantly, the position must not cause tension or pain. If you are a 'sloucher', you could take up the ideal position and then slouch back to your normal position. Somewhere in between will be right for you. Stretching and movement exercises, like those taught in yoga classes, are ideal to prepare your body for a good meditation posture.

Ideal Lying Position

Lie on your back with your head on a cushion or pillow to keep your neck as straight as possible. Have your arms by your side, preferably with your palms facing up. Have your legs next to one another with your feet falling out slightly. Make sure you are comfortable. If you have a lower back problem you may find it helpful to have a cushion under your knees. Use a blanket if you cannot keep warm otherwise.

Other Preliminaries

It is best to have your eyes closed for each exercise. If you find that difficult, you may want to start off with your eyes half-closed. You may find that you sometimes fall asleep with the exercises. This is fine if you use the relaxation to help you go to sleep. Otherwise, try to stay awake to get the full physical and psychological benefit from your practice. All the exercises are teaching you skills that you will be able to use in your life.

While doing the exercises you may have all sorts of unrelated thoughts come into your mind. Do not fight them or get angry with yourself. Just acknowledge those interfering thoughts and let them go. The exercises *Body, Feelings, Mind* and *Positive Thinking* in this pack will help you distance yourself from your thoughts.

Using the Programme

Repeated practice is essential with all the exercises. Do not be discouraged if a particular exercise appears too difficult or does not seem to help. Try several times. With repeated practice some of the skills taught in the exercises will become part of you, and you can use them even when you are not listening to the tape.

For most people the two relaxation exercises, *Muscular Relaxation* (cassette A, side 1) and *Relaxed Breathing* (cassette A, side 2) are the most appropriate starting point. Some people prefer one rather than the other. Find out which one suits you best. Then practise it regularly every day. Most people find morning or evening best for the practice. If both relaxation exercises work for you, use them on alternate days. Both exercises will teach you the skill to relax very quickly out there in the world when you feel stressed or anxious.

The exercise *Meditation (Body, Feelings, Mind)* (cassette B, side 1) will deepen your relaxation practice and it can also teach you to connect with your 'inner sanctuary'. It is a very powerful exercise for some people, and you should always allow sufficient time for it. Use this exercise only after you have practised the previous relaxation exercises for a while.

Use *Concentration, Positive Thinking* (cassette B, side 2) if your anxiety or stress has a large 'mental' component, that is, it is often triggered or made worse by your thoughts. The exercise will teach you to distance yourself from your negative thoughts and invite positive thoughts into your mind.

The exercise *Evaluation* (cassette C, side 1) will help you evaluate and learn from anxiety or stress provoking situations. Use it after you have had a 'bad time'. You will be guided through the experience to learn from it and to handle similar situations differently in future.

Preparation (Cassette C, side 2) should be used before you are facing a stressful or anxiety-provoking situation. It will help prevent the build-up of anticipatory anxiety, and you will develop an appropriate 'coping strategy' instead.

Caution

It is really important that you never listen to any of the exercises on the tapes while you are doing something that requires your full attention such as driving your car. Make uninterrupted time for your practice. If you are or have been receiving treatment for mental or psychological problems, especially mental illness, it is recommended that you discuss using the tapes with your doctor or psychological therapist. Deep psychological work like the exercises on these tapes can sometimes bring up strong thoughts, images or feelings. If that happens, you may need to do some work with a counsellor or psychotherapist. Your doctor is probably the best person to advise.

These exercises are well tested and have helped many people in their self-development. However, they cannot replace counselling, psychotherapy or medical treatment.

Further Reading and Listening

The following books are excellent if you want to further explore the wider context of life.

Kowalski R, 1987, *Over the Top*, Winslow, Bicester. (Out of print.)
Kowalski R, 1993, *Discovering Your Self*, Routledge, London and New York.
Swimme B, 1996, *The Hidden Heart of the Cosmos*, Orbis Books, Mary Knoll, New York.
Talbot M, 1991, *The Holographic Universe*, HarperCollins, New York.

The following (all available from Winslow) will teach you more skills in the area of relaxation and meditation.

Bailey R, 1986, *Systematic Relaxation*, Winslow, Bicester. (cassette & user's manual.)
Kowalski R, Lidiard L & Jones S, 1997, *Relaxation Tools CD*, Joliko, Maidenhead.
Simmons M & Daw P, 1994, *Stress, Anxiety, Depression*, Winslow, Bicester. (A practical workbook.)